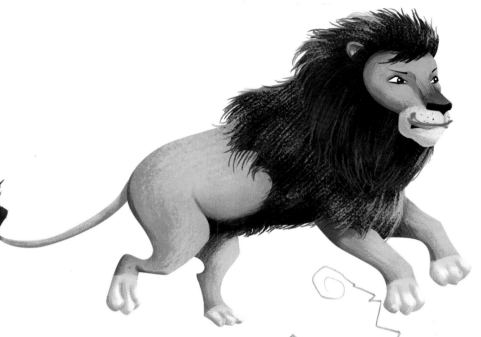

This book belongs to

_____

Written by Tapasi De
Illustrated by Suman S. Roy

Lions are known as the 'king of the jungle'.

Lions live in grasslands, savanna or open woodlands.

Lions are found in Asia and Africa.

A female lion is called a 'lioness' and a baby lion is called a 'cub'.

Male lions have a mane of hair around their heads.

A lion's roar can be heard from far away.

A group of lions is called a 'pride'.

In a pride, the lionesses hunt.

A lion makes many sounds like snarling, hissing, coughing, miaowing, woofing and roaring.

A lion can see five times better than a human being.

Lions have a tufted tail.

Lions can run very fast.

These large cats can
drink a lot of water.

Most lions live for around 13 years.

Lions rest up to 16-20 hours each day!

New words to learn

family

Asia

Africa

females

pride

tufted

snarling

hissing

coughing

miaowing

woofing

roaring